D1536146

Who Sold My Cheese?

A *sharp* little book for anyone who wants
to become an expert at relationship based sales,
without all the *cheesy stuff*!

Kirk and Mary Kjellberg

Who Sold My Cheese?

Kirk and Mary Kjellberg

For more information about this book, other available
products or services please visit:
www.whosoldmycheese.com

or contact us at:

e-mail: info@whosoldmycheese.com

763-688-1628, 10a.m. to 6p.m. (Central Time)

ISBN: 978-09819448-0-7

Book Design by: www.KarrieRoss.com

Disclaimer: All characters and locations in this book are fiction-
al. Any resemblances to persons living or dead is purely
coincidental.

Who Sold My Cheese?

DEDICATION

This book is dedicated to my wife Mary. Her unwavering support for the idea of making this book a reality has in time made it so. Without her, it would just be another idea floating in the sea of ideas that occupies my mind. Her ability to gently herd me toward a conclusion is something I will cherish as long as I live.

A dedication for a relationship-based sales book would not be complete without mentioning my Father, Kent. I grew up in his sales business and always saw the value of building relationships with the customer and treating them like a friend.

Special thanks to:

Sarah Edwards for her guidance, patience and input. Your friendship and insight have been an inspiration.

Karrie Ross, our book designer, for picking up the pieces and helping mend the vision BS left behind. We appreciate you.

Oliver Wilder for capturing our vision for the illustration of Ben on the cover.

TABLE OF CONTENTS

How this Book was Born

My sister was locked in a dead end job in the hospitality business. She wanted to start a career in sales to make more cash and have more time with her young children. To help her prepare for this change I sent her several of the most popular books on selling. She later told me she would rather eat worms than read them as they were very dry and mechanical by nature.

Sales can be a sometimes intricate process which needed to be demystified. Having been in sales my entire working life I decided it was time to put selling into its proper context, a relationship building process combined with an easy to read easy to remember format, story-form.

If you're in need of a new career or extra income, use this book to gain a complete understanding of sales. Please consider reading this book more than once while you practice the lessons presented within it.

Best of luck in all your endeavors, and keep in mind we offer professional consulting, coaching, onsite training and keynote speeches to enhance your success.

Contact Kirk Kjellberg at 763-688-1628 weekdays between 10am and 6pm (Central Time) or email whosoldmycheese@gmail.com for more information.

From Chef to Sales, Sonja Goes to School

It was the second time in Sonja's life that she had been in an incubator. Born premature, she spent nearly three months in one and had struggled throughout her youth trying to play catch up, always feeling one step behind in her interactions with her peers. She had one all-time favorite song verse by Alan Jackson she sang to herself whenever she got to feeling small, "Well, it's alright to be little bitty, little hometown or a big old city. Might as well share, might as well smile, life goes on for a little bitty while..."

Early on, her determination and brains earned her a 4.0 graduation with a degree in business administration from Argosy University. Shortly after graduation, Sonja realized she wanted to follow her dream of being a chef and someday owning her own catering business. She began work as an apprentice with Ella's Catering in San Francisco, where she excelled with her designs and creativity.

However, the behavior of the head chef at Ella's was simply rude and demanding, if not demeaning. "Speak only when spoken to" was the unwritten rule.

Seeing no real future at Ella's, she packed up and moved north to continue her education at the Culinary Institute of America's West Coast campus, nestled deep in the Napa Valley, where she graduated with honors.

After graduation she headed back south to work as a sous-chef in some of Los Angeles's top restaurants. This gave her some much needed "flesh" for her resume, but lowered her spirits. Just like at Ella's, the executive chefs of these hot spots acted like B-list celebrities who had forgotten where they had come from. It seemed that "demanding and demeaning" was some kind of theme in the restaurant business.

In the real world of being a chef, things were much tougher and more competitive than she had ever imagined. Now, at twenty-nine years of age, she had a new set of challenges requiring the assistance of an incubator once again. With her parents' support including a commercial loan approval letter from their Bank, and her slender savings account at stake, she set out to open her own catering business, called *Gran Alimento*, (Spanish for "great food").

Because she lacked any practical business operation experience, the approval of her loan came with a condition. She would have to be selected to participate in a special Small Business Incubator program at the University of Southern California. Sonja was really ready to get things cooking, so she didn't completely understand the need for this requirement.

The tuition for this program would cost a lot of money, and participating in the program for twelve long months would take a lot of her time. Why did she need all this? She already knew how a catering business was run, didn't she? It was, however, a requirement of her loan, so she submitted her application and waited.

Each year only twelve future entrepreneurs were hand-picked from a great many applicants to participate in the Incubator. This was done through careful examination of their résumés, academic history, and particularly by the content of an essay they had to submit detailing the reasons they should be considered.

Sonja's application stood out right away, but not for the usual reasons. In writing their essays, most students seemed to work diligently to feedback what they thought the professor wanted to hear, but not Sonja.

Professor Peter Crawford referred to applications like hers as a *miniskirt,* because the language used in the essay just barely covered up what the student didn't want to publicly reveal. Sonja's contempt for the program was nearly palpable. That kind of *who needs school, let's just make things happen* attitude reminded Peter of himself, fifteen years prior. After very careful consideration by Peter, Sonja barely made the cut.

The first several months of the program focused on general accounting and a business curriculum. It helped Sonja accomplish all of the leg work of creating her business cards and forms, and all of the necessary items for setting up her office.

Sonja had already catered a small party for her parents' thirtieth wedding anniversary and a wedding reception for her mother's friend's daughter. She had managed to work through all the kinks, and both events were a great success. Once she accomplished all of that, however, Sonja's focus became all about getting paying customers!

Incubator students had to make sales forecasts and profit projections with a timeline for accomplishing them. After the first six months of the year, Sonja was 87 percent below her projections, which were very conservative to begin with. Professor Crawford was trying to be reassuring, but also realistic. He was continually amazed at the sheer number of students who believed **build it and they will come** was an actual business philosophy! "Sonja, if your sales numbers don't improve, *your business will die!*", he told her at one point As sobering as his comments were, they were definitely a call to action.

Sonja had always had great contempt for the idea of being a salesperson, even proudly posting a "No Soliciting" sign on the door of her office. Yet now she had to find a way to generate sales. With Professor Crawford's warning about her dream dying, she swallowed her pride and went off to the bookstore to look for a book on how to sell.

She looked through the entire business section and found there were a great many books about selling. They all seemed very dry, hard to follow, and totally geared toward career salespeople exactly the kind of people who used exactly the kind of methods she so disliked.

As she was just about to leave the store empty handed, Sonja spotted a cute little book called *Who Sold My Cheese*. The intro stated that it was designed for small business owners and other professionals who were brand new to the sales role, a role they had never prepared for or expected to find themselves playing.

The book was written in story form, so understanding and applying the techniques was easy. Sonja was especially glad to learn that there was nothing tricky or underhanded about *professional, relationship-based selling*. After reading the first few chapters, Sonja began to understand that the success of her business wasn't predicated only on how well she could cook or cater, but relied heavily on her abilities to sell. Her sales numbers would really be what would make or break *Gran Alimento*.

Every year the incubator always held a sales contest, complete with a very cool prize package of office equipment and a laptop computer with all the latest software for prospecting and accounting. With the help of this new book, the sales contest now seemed possible to win and Sonja dug deeper to win the contest. Several weeks of reading, studying, and applying the lessons from this little book had profound effects. Sonja was amused at the coincidence of this book being small but powerful, just like she was.

Another participant in the program, Jan Sterlington, who had left a sales career with a Fortune 100 company to start an organic pet products company, had been at the top of the sales board since the contest began. "As it should be," Jan thought proudly. Yet as the end of the sales contest neared, she could not believe what she was seeing on the board.

She had seen Sonja's numbers climbing steadily, but she never expected they'd be nearly tied with only two months left. Jan had her heart set on the prize package too and considered winning it to be a cinch. After all, she was a career salesperson who had taken advantage of all the sales training available to her over the years.

At graduation, the graduates gathered in Peter's sizeable off-campus office for a reception and awards ceremony. For the last thirty days of the contest, the sales numbers had been kept a secret until the completion of the program to maintain the focus on learning instead of competing. When the contest results were read, Jan sank deep into her chair. Sonja had won! She had surpassed her sales projections by a whopping 37 percent! That was a 114 percent increase in sales in only six months! Since posting her sales figures at six months, Sonja had sold an additional $373,000 in bookings for weddings and several huge corporate events.

As the graduates gathered around Sonja to congratulate her, the buzz soon turned from congratulations to curiosity. Jim, who was building a truck accessory business, was impressed with her achievements, but also a bit skeptical about the big turnaround. "How could a shrinking violet like you make this kind of change in your sales numbers so quickly?" he asked. "I had all but counted you out of even surviving the course!"

"Funny you should ask," Sonja said with a huge grin. In the spirit of the holiday season Sonja had gift-wrapped twelve copies of *Who Sold My Cheese*, one for each of the eleven other members of the incubator, plus one for the Small Business Incubator's library. Moving to the back corner of the room, Sonja opened the closet door to grab a big red felt Santa sack Peter had allowed her to stash there the previous day and began to hand them out.

As the graduates unwrapped their books, they all chuckled at the title, except Jan.

"Sales is a serious business, not some kind of joke," Jan pointedly commented.

"Yes, it is serious," said Sonja, "but it has to be fun and fulfilling too, and that is exactly the difference this little book made for me."

"A $373,000 difference," Jim chimed in, bringing huge laughs from the group.

Sonja said, "This book has been the difference between life and death for my dream of being an independent businesswoman. That's serious enough for me!" Sonja then asked each person to agree to read the book before New Year's Eve. She offered to cater a big party for the group just after winter break when they would not only share in her victory, but also discuss the outcome of their reading.

Sonja's fellow classmates Tony and Sarah were busy talking together during Sonja's invitation, so Peter asked in his best singsong teacher voice, "Is there something you two would like to share with the whole class?"

"Why, yes, there is," Sarah said. "We shouldn't wait until after break to begin! This is a pretty small book. If we each read some of it aloud, it would be good public speaking practice and we could use some of these newfound skills tomorrow!"

A unanimous agreement rang out through the class, and Peter's giant black leather desk chair was brought to the front of the group. Electing to go first, Sonja began reading the first chapter aloud…

BEN LEARNS TO SELL, OR ELSE!

Ben Porterfield runs the most profitable dairy farm and cheese factory in all of Wisconsin. You wouldn't know it from looking at him. His tall, muscular body, which is constantly draped in blue overalls that are too big for him, his boyish grin, and round spectacles make him look like a college professor who got lost in the backcountry.

Not only is the farm large and profitable, but its six hundred acres of rolling hills in Springfield Corners are so beautiful they often appear in photo contests and on the cover of local calendars. Porterfield's Limburger, Cheddar and Gouda cheeses have won a great many contests. The walls of Ben's den are covered with ribbons and trophies.

Considering how successful the farm is today, it is funny to look back to the time not long after

Ben inherited the farm from his father George, when a recession, combined with Ben's inability to sell his products left the farm on the brink of bankruptcy. Even today Ben thinks back often to the time his dad had decided to take a huge chance by adding a cheese-making facility to the farm and began making his award-winning cheeses.

George had built the operation into a profitable business and had added on to the factory twice over the years. Together he and Ben used to haul their cheeses far and wide. To "Green Bay and Beyond" George would shout as he and Ben pulled from the driveway. Ben had enjoyed these trips with his father immensely, but because he was rather reserved in nature, he could never get used to the goings-on of the farmer's markets or the stops at the local cheese shops with all the "wheeling and dealing" that the selling of cheese entailed. George had convinced Ben that "wheeling and dealing" stood for selling wheels of cheese! "My dad was such a colorful character", Ben later recalled.

Ben loved the processes of milking cows and hand-crafting the finest cheeses, but he truly "couldn't sell his way out of a wet paper bag," as his Dad had put it. Ben was painfully shy and after his father had died he continued to suffer through the farmers markets in Green Bay but eventually, watching sales drop, he knew he had to find another way.

Fate brought that *other way* to Ben when Tommy Shepper came calling on a hot June afternoon to tell Ben that he had just started a new business as a cheese broker! "Hallelujah!" Ben exclaimed. He quickly agreed to give Tommy a 12 percent commission in exchange for his handling the sales end of things. Twelve percent is a very small price to pay to have someone else handle all of that sales crap, Ben thought cheerfully. No more road trips, cold calling or negotiating for Ben, just glorious cheese making forevermore!

Tommy kept the orders coming, and took very good care of them both for all of fifteen years until one day Tommy just up and died. His tombstone read, "Tommy had a gouda heart, may he rest in pizza,"

Once Ben's initial shock and grief began to ebb, fear took its place. *"What am I to do with all this years' perfectly aged cheese just waiting here for*

Tommy's skillful tongue to turn it into cash?" Ben's worrisome thoughts continued. *"There soon would be no room on the aging racks for all the new cheese that's being made?"*

He quickly began to look high and low for a guy like Tommy who could handle the sales end of things, but to no avail. Consolidation had made the cheese business a dreadfully cutthroat industry.

Furthermore, Super Cheese Distributors, LLC had completely taken over the wholesaling end of the business. This company was not well liked by most of the farmers they bought product from, so when Super Cheese agreed to see him, Ben was both excited and quite wary.

During the first ten minutes of their meeting, the representatives at Super Cheese told Ben, "You're too much into all that specialty cheese, so we don't know how much of it we can move. We take a 40 percent commission on the sales volume and we will give you no promises as to volume."

"Forty percent of the sales my butt!" Ben snorted as he milked the cows. Super Cheese's business philosophies just made him angry. "I hate salesmen!" he roared. The *stupid salesmen* who came by the farm usually left as fast as they came in because Ben frequently just headed out into the manure-filled barnyard, ignoring their attempts to persuade him to buy their products.

Ben remembered one particular salesman with a smile. He had relentlessly tried to maneuver Ben into buying his product and wouldn't take *no* for an answer. He was finally *helped* to leave the farm with the business end of a pitchfork poking him in the backside.

"I don't know anything about all that sales stuff," Ben said aloud, "but someone has to sell this cheese. There has to be a way out of this mess." All of a sudden Ben leapt into the air right there in the barn and yelled, "I am going to be the best dang cheese salesman in all of Wisconsin!" The poor cows nearly jumped right out of their stanchions, while the word "salesman" just hung there in the air, like a fart in church. Somehow Ben just knew he could not be a conventional salesman.

On Ben's walk down to the barn the following morning, he had some interesting thoughts. His father had never acted like a salesman; in fact, he had been nothing like the idiots at Super Cheese or the jerks that came calling at the farm. As Ben reflected on his situation, his intuition started to emerge. Ben had a hunch that the answers to the dilemmas he currently faced in his life, would be found in the old trunk his dad had left behind. He decided it was high time to act on that hunch.

The trunk was full of old journals George had kept since he started farming. Ben had looked at them briefly after George's passing but he hadn't actually read any of them. Now Ben's inner voice was telling him it was time to go through those old journals page by page. He was going to take a vacation to do just that, he decided. Following another course of action would be a welcome change.

It was early spring in Wisconsin, still well too cold and wet to plant, and that meant no shortage of able-bodied help to run the farm for a few days. With arrangements for the care of the farm made, Ben loaded his father's old trunk into the car. As he approached the Wind Walker Lodge, just the sight of the sign brought a big smile to Ben's face. Images of rare and very memorable summertime childhood vacations at this lodge were still etched deeply in Ben's mind.

Once Ben had checked in and settled into his cozy room over looking Rose Lake, he began to sort out and read through the journals one at a time. What he found on those pages totally shocked him. From his reading, Ben discovered that his father had been as unsure about how to sell his prized cheeses as Ben was now. The journals not only detailed all of George's fears and worries from the day he purchased the farm, but also detailed his every action taken to overcome those fears.

Ben had never imagined that his father could have been so unsure about anything, let alone how to sell. But now, as he read through the journals, he saw just how simple overcoming his own fears of selling could be.

One quotation that said it all leapt off the page and made perfect sense to Ben:

"<u>Everyone</u> is in sales.
No matter what you do for
a living, you do need to sell.
Sell yourself, your ideas,
your products, even
your dreams."
—*Unknown*

As Ben read further into the journals he realized that neither his own fears, nor his father's, were about making a great product. Instead, both of their concerns related to fears about how to sell that product!

Each new section of the old journals revealed different aspects of George's education about the sales process. Ben had mistakenly thought salesmanship was just some kind of *you have it or you don't thing* that his dad seemed to have been born with. Never in a million years would Ben have imagined that learning such simple philosophies and taking straightforward action steps relating to sales, had insured the growth and success of the farm. As Ben continued to read through the journals, George's warm feelings of love and connection to the farm flowed freely on the pages.

Ben had always known that his dad had loved the farm, but he had never realized how his father had struggled to change it in the face of changing times and opportunities after World War II. After several relaxing days at the lodge, Ben separated out the sales journals from the rest of the contents of the trunk and decided it was time to head back home and begin to use the sales process his father had mastered many long years ago.

When Ben got home, he headed straight for the barn. Once there, he quickly decided to paint a large wall in the milk house with a fresh coat of white paint and make it into a huge chalkboard. With five gallons of white paint and a few adjustments in lighting, Ben soon had his classroom. Using a king-size black magic marker, Ben wrote his very first lesson from the journals on the wall:

> "IN THE MODERN WORLD
> OF BUSINESS, IT IS USELESS
> TO BE A CREATIVE ORIGINAL
> THINKER UNLESS YOU
> CAN ALSO SELL WHAT
> YOU CREATE."
> –DAVID M. OGILVY

"I do so enjoy the creativity of running the cheese factory," Ben thought. Then he shuddered at the image of the bankrupt factory in mothballs. The very first lesson on the chalkboard raced back into his mind; "Unless you can also sell what you create." "If I can't sell what we create, the farm will die!" Ben said aloud.

The first thing Ben decided to do was to call on Tommy's widow, Susan, to see about getting Tommy's contacts from her, but to no avail. The owner of Super Cheese Distributors had just signed the deal with Susan to buy Tommy's entire business from her. After hearing Ben's request, Susan said softly, "Ben, if I had thought for one moment that **_you_** would be interested in sales, I would have sold to you for a lot less."

"How am I going to know who to call on now?" Ben said aloud after hanging up the phone.

The journals pointed to prospecting as the first step in the sales process. Without prospects Ben had nowhere to start. As he sat reading in his living room, the phone rang. It was his nephew Willy. Willy had been spending summers with Ben since he was six years old. Now a senior at Kaplan College in Milwaukee, he had become quite an asset to the business. Hearing what Ben wanted to accomplish as far as prospecting, Willy told Ben to load the fax machine with paper and get a good night's sleep!

In the morning Ben couldn't believe his eyes. Willy had sent over sixty pages, each filled with the phone numbers and addresses of specialty cheese shops and the names of buyers for upscale grocers across America. The fax machine was incessantly beeping until Ben reloaded the paper and even more pages shot out!

Ben noticed that the pages all came from different Internet sites. "*www.how-old-school-am-I.com?*" Ben thought as he started to haul the stacks of old phone books he had been planning to use for prospecting out to the dumpster.

Later that evening the phone rang. It was Willy. "What did you think about the lists I sent you?" he asked.

After a long conversation with his excited nephew, Ben was so glad to have his help that he soon turned the talk to his plan to promote Willy as soon as he graduated. After Ben finished his phone call with Willy and reviewed the hundreds of contacts on the lists Willy had sent to him, he walked out to the barn and up to the chalkboard and wrote:

"PROSPECTS = POSSIBLITIES
PERIOD."

TO THRIVE IN SALES I MUST
HAVE A LARGE AND GROWING
DATA BASE OF CUSTOMERS TO
CONTACT. WITH TECHNOLOGY
TODAY, THERE IS NO LIMIT TO
THE AVAILABLE STREAM
OF DATA. IN TODAY'S WORLD,
UTILIZING TECHNOLOGY IS
ESSENTIAL TO PROPER
PROSPECTING.

THE FIRST AND MOST
IMPORTANT STEP IN SELLING
IS PROSPECTING. IT IS THE
MOST IMPORTANT, BECAUSE
IF I HAVE NO ONE TO TALK
TO, I CAN'T GET ANY
NEW CUSTOMERS!

Willy had used the company credit card to purchase good and up-to-date prospecting lists. Ben had protested the costs, citing the phone book and other free sources of information.

"It takes twice as much time to sort the junk out of those free sources, and after all, *time is money, Uncle*!" Willy had said this with a huge laugh. Ben remembered using this same saying **many times** to get Willy to understand the processes around the farm and factory.

In the coming days Ben learned that there were a great many ways to prospect. There were prospecting lists for sale, trade publications to research, and Internet yellow pages available for his use as well. Ben compared prospecting every day to placing daily deposits into a savings account that could then compound the results of those efforts. *GOOD PROSPECTS = GOOD POSSIBILITES*, he reminded himself daily.

On Monday morning Ben decided to get started making phone calls. As he sat down at his desk Ben thought, *"This will be easy."* Then something interesting happened as he started to pick up the phone. Ben's palms started to sweat and his breathing got shallow. He was as nervous as a school kid asking for a prom date.

There were forty names on the first list, and as he worked his way down the list a funny thing occurred. Just as he had pictured, Ben heard a variety of responses; "We don't want any," "We already have a regular supplier," "Where did you get this number?" There were also some that had no answer at all or an answering machine, a few more who said, "Please send us something in the mail," there was one hang up and finally there were those who said, "Yes, we can set up an appointment."

Ben was exhausted. He felt let down, rejected, and deflated. "This sucks!" he said aloud. Then he took a look outside. His factory workers were on a break talking with the farm hands and they were all having a good laugh. The warm sun of spring had burnt off the haze and was shining brightly on the rolling hills. It revitalized Ben. He took a long sip of coffee and studied the list he had worked on.

He took out his calculator. "In the end, the total was six appointments out of forty calls, that's not an 85 percent failure rate, that's a 15 percent success rate!" He also noticed that the further down the list he got, the better his odds became at getting an appointment because his way of asking for the appointment had vastly improved. *"While it's very human to look only at the 85 percent failure rate, I need to focus on the 15 percent in the positive column"*, Ben thought.

Remembering the trip to Las Vegas he had taken for a break from winter last year, he sat back and thought of the casinos. If anyone understood statistics and odds, it was the casinos. Then he thought about the phone calls that had gone badly. *"This isn't personal, it's mathematical, it's all about the odds,"* he thought. He stood up, stretched, and walked out to the barn to use the chalkboard and wrote:

USE MATHEMATICS TO KEEP YOURSELF ON TRACK IN YOUR PROSPECTING. IT'S A 100 PERCENT HUMAN TENDENCY TO TRY AND AVOID BEING REJECTED. THIS IS THE KEY PLACE WHERE SO MANY WHO ARE NEW TO SALES WILL FALL DOWN BECAUSE THEY TAKE IT PERSONALLY.

HAVING SOMEONE SAY NO DURING PROSPECTING CAN SIMPLY MEAN THEY ARE TOO BUSY, ARE HAVING SOME BIG PROBLEMS OF THEIR OWN, OR THEY SIMPLY DON'T TRUST PEOPLE THEY DO NOT KNOW. THEY MAY ALSO SIMPLY LOVE THE VENDOR OR PERSON THAT THEY ARE NOW USING. IT'S NOT REJECTION, IT'S STATISTICS AT WORK.

By treating prospecting just like a study of the odds, Ben easily rationalized that any rejection faced was truly statistical and not personal. *"How could they be rejecting me personally when they don't know me personally? When someone says no, statistically this means I am simply one call closer to receiving a yes."* Ben thought.

Ben had to smile at how simple his dad had made prospecting seem in a quote from his journal: "SW – SW – SW - SW" which translated to, "Some will, some won't, so what, someone's waiting!"

Depending on the nature of the business, it was usually beneficial to take a more casual approach to introducing oneself over the phone. Once Ben reached the person he wanted to speak with, he would use the exact same script each time: "Hello. My name is Ben with Porterfield Cheese and I would like to send you a free sample of an award winning cheese of your choice. Would you like to hear your choices?" His dad always called this the "mouse approach," because when the prospects smelled free cheese they just had to check it out!

Lessons from the journals came back to Ben's mind:

> *When you're new to dialing for dollars, it's best if you have an approach that offers a giveaway. If that's not possible, creating an opening line that stirs interest takes practice. By all means, lean toward the outlandish as opposed to boring.*

In Ben's understanding of the journals lessons, once you have gained the appointment, the next step in the process was to conduct research about the potential customer. In these information rich days, a mouse click or two could tell volumes about a prospect. Yet there is no substitute for asking good questions.

Ben's mind rang with the lessons of the journals once again:

> *Even if the scene is set in a retail setting, the process looks much the same. Asking good questions and learning how you may be of service to the prospect is paramount to the sales process.*

*Serving the customer is what sepa-
rates peddlers from salespeople. Peddlers
have something to unload. Anyone will do
as a prospect. They are solely interested in
talking the prospect into buying what
they have to sell and then they are long
gone. Thus the bad rap most people place
on salespeople.*

The journals continued:

*In contrast, sales-based relationships
are much different because they are built on
trust. A true salesperson can't browbeat
someone into having a long-term relationship with him; the prospect has to want the
relationship as much as the salesperson.
Building sales-based relationships comes
from careful attention to a certain set of steps
taken over a period of time to determine how
to "BE OF SERVICE" to the customer.*

Deciding it was time for a stretch; Ben walked
down to the milk house and wrote his current
thoughts on the wall.

SELLING IS THE ART OF INTRODUCING PEOPLE TO PRODUCTS OR SERVICES IN SUCH A WAY THAT ALLOWS THEM TO ENHANCE THEIR LIVES. GREAT SALESPEOPLE DON'T HAVE TO CREATE A NEED BECAUSE THEIR CUSTOMERS HAVE NEEDS ALREADY!

GREAT SALESPEOPLE SIMPLY FIND A WAY TO FILL AN EXISTING NEED WHILE CREATING A RELATIONSHIP THAT INVITES REFERRALS AND REPEAT BUSINESS.

Once Ben had a short list of appointments with prospects to go and visit he became much more chipper about the whole process of calling on customers. It was time to put some of these theories into practice.

As if guided by his father's memory, Ben filled some of the same crates his dad had used for the trips they had taken together with perfectly aged samples of their best selections. At dawn he gassed up his dad's old Buick Roadmaster station wagon and headed east on route 164. Ben shouted, "To Green Bay and beyond!" as he left the farm, laughing so hard he had tears in his eyes.

As an oldies station came into range, the music set him daydreaming about his father and thinking about all things "wheeling and dealing." His memories of those times were surprisingly clear. In his day, his father had made many more pounds of cheese than Ben did now and was still sold out every year, despite there being much fewer folks around to buy it at the time. "All I have to do is exactly as my dad did," Ben said aloud.

As he remembered the farmers' market scene that had always seemed so competitive, it reminded him of his own wheeling and dealing in Springfield Corners. He had negotiated hardware store orders, used tractors from Joe at the implement dealership, pickup trucks from the Chevy dealer, and all manner of other things. In looking back, they had all been good-hearted conversations in which all parties either got what they wanted out of the deal or simply agreed to disagree. In a town the size of Springfield Corners, the locals only did *for people*, never *to them*. What a great way to think about selling, to only do things that are beneficial *for* your customers!

Just as Ben had run all these thoughts through his mind seemingly a million times, he spotted a specialty cheese shop just ahead. While this shop was not one of his appointed stops, he decided to do as his dad had done so often before. He would use the *mouse approach* by just leaving some cheese with the store owners to see if they liked it, then he'd check back sometime later.

It was during this first daring sales call that he encountered an absolutely captivating woman named Vernie Hollis. It was very early spring, so the shop was completely empty as Ben strolled in. She saw that he was carrying a box and was quick to point to the "No Soliciting" sign posted over the cash register.

Ben just laughed and said, "I'm not selling anything."

"Oh, so you're here to buy something then?" Vernie asked in a slightly challenging tone.

"Why, yes, I believe I could use some summer sausage to go with this," he said tapping the box in his hand.

Ben was instantly, inexplicably, and completely drawn to this stunning woman. She was reserved, yet feisty. As they talked, she began to soften a bit and Ben was able to ask her some questions about some of the different cheeses she had for sale. It became clear to her that Ben really knew his cheese very well.

"All right, cowboy, what's with the box?" Vernie asked jokingly while gazing at Ben.

He simply told her that it was a free sample of the world famous Porterfield Wisconsin White Cheddar.

"Porterfield?" she said with her nose all wrinkled up.

"Why do you say it that way?" Ben asked, smiling.

"That Porterfield guy is a big jerk from what I've heard," Vernie said. "I buy from Sam over at Super Cheese Distributors and he told me that Porterfield thinks his products are just way too good for regular shops like mine."

"Well, his being a **big jerk** aside, what do you think of his cheeses?" Ben asked.

"I don't know I never have tried any of them," Vernie replied.

Ben quickly wrapped up his conversation with Vernie, paying for his sausage selection and a soda on his way out. He was half way out the door when he realized he still had the sample box in his hand. "Here, this is for you I have more in the car," he said, smiling. Leaving the box on the counter for Vernie, Ben walked out the door saying," You have a good day now."

Vernie quickly opened the box out of curiosity and darn near died of embarrassment right there on the spot.

The note card taped to the cheese sample said, *Simply the best cheese you've ever tasted guaranteed, Ben Porterfield.* There was no mistaking she had just insulted an industry icon as it had been Willy's idea to place Ben's picture on the card as well.

She bolted to the parking lot only to see the old Roadmaster putting rubber to the road and Ben yelling out the window, "to Green Bay and beyond!" as he drove out of sight.

Ben was thinking of this trip as *rolling research* of sorts, so he stopped at all the shops on his list of appointments and many other shops he saw along the way. He found that, no matter what the outcome, there was a mathematical equation at work.

Most people were nice, some were not. The bottom line was that a percentage of people bought and a percentage of them didn't. "*Mathematics at work, just as I suspected,*" Ben thought.

Ben's rolling research was the most fun he had had in a great many years. As he made his way through Wisconsin he decided to roll into Green Bay to buy himself a new laptop computer. He also bought the software he would need to keep track of all the prospects he had met, as well as all the gear necessary to get hooked up to the Internet.

Once he returned to the farm, Ben stayed up until midnight setting up his computer and learning the prospecting software. The next day Ben got a few pointers from Willy and set up a wireless network at home and even in the barn! Ben thought, "*For a guy who didn't know a modem from a hole in the ground, I think I did pretty well!*" Ben hadn't been this happy and excited about anything in as long as he could remember.

Ben was soon surfing up a storm on the web. For the first time Ben actually saw his own web site on his own laptop and was totally thrilled. Willy had not only built the site, but answered all e-mails and had simply faxed Ben anything that needed his attention. Now Willy had set up an e-mail account for Ben as well.

Ben just couldn't believe that he already had his first e-mail. "It's a forwarded message from me Uncle, you didn't win the lottery!" Willy said jokingly about Ben's unbridled enthusiasm over the e-mail's arrival in his inbox. The forwarded e-mail was from vernie@hollyhillsfarms.com.

Forgetting all about Willy, Ben's pulse quickened remembering the Holly Hills wrapper on that fantastic summer sausage he had bought at Vernie's shop. Opening the e-mail, Ben laughed at the outpouring of embarrassment written there. As Ben read the letter he all but forgot about still being on the phone with Willy as he read it.

"I'll have to call her," Ben said aloud, conjuring up Vernie's face in his mind.

The sound of Willy's voice in his ear brought Ben back to the present "Uncle, in today's world you text, instant message and e-mail girls, you don't *call* them," he chided.

"Well, that's nice, Willy, except I don't have an instant messenger machine."

Once Willy could catch his breath from laughing so hard, he realized how much he had yet to teach Ben. "Just click the *reply* button and type a note back to her. Send me an instant message if you have any problems, Uncle," Willy said jokingly as he hung up.

"I would really like to take her out on a date," Ben thought aloud. "How about a relationship-based sales approach?" Opening up his laptop again he was happy to see the blank reply page now. "*I need to get an appointment with her,*" he now thought. But then he thought, "*Well, I don't know anything about her or her shop and I should.*" So he opened up his web browser and *Googled* her.

He read all about her shop and, how it was now being run by a third generation of the Hollis family, and then he clicked on the "about us" button.

There Vernie was standing proudly in front of the store with her grandmother and father. Two other links to a local newspaper talked of her involvement in the community and her church. "*All good to know*," Ben thought.

With his research completed, he finally went back to the e-mail and simply wrote, "Dear Vernie. In my life I've been called much worse than a jerk, and that was right here on my own farm! No harm done. Can I stop by your shop on Friday to talk with you?"

It wasn't fifteen minutes later when the beeping his laptop let out said, "You've got mail!"

Nervously he opened the reply e-mail from her. "Dear Ben, Thanks for being so understanding. We're closed on Sunday; can you come up for a late breakfast after church instead?"

And so it went until the time and place was set.

Ben sat back and thought about all that had transpired. "*Relationship selling is just like dating! First*

I came across a prospect through my actions of getting out there and looking around. Then I got an appointment to meet with her to see if there is any mutual desire."

Ben was literally floating around the farm for the next few days. He couldn't thank Willy enough for teaching him about e-mails and the Internet. As he thought about why he had given up on dating, he realized it was because he had never before been able to think of it in the same light as relationship-based sales.

First and foremost you had to care and believe in what you had to offer, create a vision of the kind of person you wanted to date (perfect customer), then find potential dating partners to talk to (prospects), and devise a good way of introducing yourself to them. Ben was now applying the philosophy of *some will, some won't, so what, someone's waiting* to his personal life as well.

Ben laughed at the similarities but realized he had taken the "no thank you(s)" of asking for a date much too personally. *"It's easier to be alone than to be rejected,"* he thought. *"The fear of rejection is obviously what makes people stumble and fall in sales as well as dating."*

On that note he went out to the barn, walked up to the board and wrote:

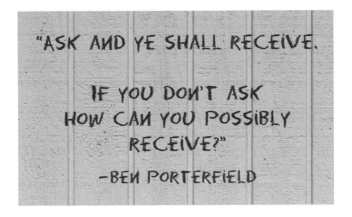

"ASK AND YE SHALL RECEIVE,

IF YOU DON'T ASK
HOW CAN YOU POSSIBLY
RECEIVE?"

–BEN PORTERFIELD

With that quote staring back at him, Ben headed back to the house and sat by the crackling fireplace with some hot spiced chai tea and immersed himself in his dad's journals once again.

George wrote: *The art of introducing one's self is worth refining and exploring. You have to be able to judge if the person you are talking to can indeed even make a decision. If they are in that capacity, is it* a convenient time for them? Are they receptive or distracted? Salespeople get so caught up in their own presentation that they forget the person they are talking to is a person with responsibilities, insecurities, car troubles, employees, children, dogs, husbands, or wives.

A great salesperson is one who **pays attention** and, is willing to reschedule, or one who simply asks how he can be of service to the prospect if it is obvious that the prospect is really in a bind. Most people don't want to ask if they can help, simply out of fear that they may actually be taken up on their invitation! When a salesperson genuinely wants to be of service, he will be very surprised at how appreciative people are when they know that he is interested in what's best for all concerned, instead of just what's best for him as the salesperson.

In order to find out how to be of service to prospects it is imperative to ask questions. There is a fundamental politeness

to asking permission to ask questions.
It sounds as simple as, "Would it be okay if
I asked you a few questions about your
business?" Interviewing someone is the easi-
est thing in the world if, as a salesperson,
you are genuinely interested in the process of
building an ongoing relationship. The term
"interview" sounds formal, yet it is simply
a series of questions designed to evaluate the
client's needs. Like any relationship, business or personal, it is necessary to see if
there is any commonality between you.

Salespeople who launch into their
presentation without benefit of taking time
for rapport building by asking good
questions or making the effort to fully
understand their clients' needs are just being
foolish and wasting everyone's time.
Potential prospects may seem guarded
at first until they are certain of the sales-
persons intentions. Be willing to gather
information without presenting any
solutions. This also builds a sense of

anticipation and interest in the prospect. Relationship-based sales is an incremental process of building trust and value. It's a marathon, not a sprint.

Aside from interviews being a useful tool for building rapport, a prospect needs to be interviewed to determine if there is a need to be filled or a pain that can be soothed by the products or services of the salesperson. It is very important to be careful and tactful in asking about the prospect's business or any problems or pains which may exist.

It is very hard for anyone to expose their personal or business shortcomings, ESPECIALLY to a total stranger. This is the other key reason that salespeople who take the time to get to know their prospects and their business will have much less resistance. Once a salesperson has defined the customer's needs by asking lots of good questions therein lies the opportunity to present solutions.

The journals were also quite specific about the steps to take in defining potential solutions and presenting those ideas to prospective clients:

> *Presenting solutions needs to follow closely along the lines of the conversation that is taking place. Treating prospects like friends is important here. Be extra sure not to try and force something on them that clearly doesn't fit their needs. If the salesperson can unquestionably see that there is not a match for his product and the prospect's needs, he must say so.*

> *Many referrals and future business can be derived from contacts that have been treated well during the presentation of solutions phase. If it is plain to see that there is not a match between the prospect and the product, the salesperson should ask for a referral immediately. It is a small world, and if the salesperson has been considerate and thoughtful, the prospect may very well refer a friend or family member.*

As Ben sat thinking about all he had read, an old saying came to mind: "The brain can only absorb what the butt can withstand." And with that he got up from his chair, took a big stretch and walked down to the barn to record a few thoughts and lessons before he locked up for the night.

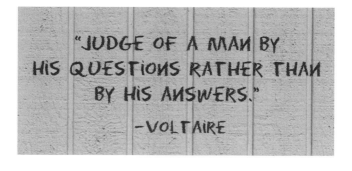

"JUDGE OF A MAN BY HIS QUESTIONS RATHER THAN BY HIS ANSWERS."

—VOLTAIRE

PRESENT SOLUTIONS iN A PALATABLE WAY. PRESENTING A SOLUTION USING LANGUAGE THAT iS CONSTRUCTIVE iN NATURE MAKES THE PROSPECT WANT TO GET iNVOLVED iN THE SOLUTIONS YOU ARE DESCRIBING.

USE DESCRIPTIONS OF GROWTH OR ENJOYMENT SO THAT THE PROSPECT CAN EASILY iMAGINE THE BENEFITS OF WHAT YOU ARE PRESENTING.

When Ben came to the part of the journals about asking for a commitment, (a trial close), he could tell from his own reaction that this was the part of selling that caused the most anxiety in the hearts and minds of salespeople.

Ben looked back over his own notes and noticed how far he had advanced down the list of steps to conduct a sale:

- Prospecting
- Introduction
- Interview / evaluation of needs / (what, where, when, why?)
- Defining potential solutions
- Presenting ideas and solutions about products or services when appropriate

It was in the *asking for a commitment* part that Ben noticed tightness in his gut and, shortness in his breath, even though he was still just sitting in the living room. *"Wow, this closing stuff brings up strong emotions!"* Ben thought.

In thinking all this over, Ben remembered a fascinating statistic he had read on the Internet about closing a sale: fully sixty percent of professional sales people **fail to ever even ask for the order**!

"No wonder there is such a difference between the salespeople who perform and those who barely scrape along," Ben

thought. Once again he remembered a journal quote about asking for a commitment: *If a salesperson asks for the order and the prospect tells him no, did he lose anything? The answer is: of course not. If he didn't have the order when he asked and he doesn't have it now, he is exactly the same, not in any way less or somehow damaged!*

The journals continued with great lessons about overcoming objections:

Salespeople have another mental hurdle to jump and that is the ever dreaded objection. To put a twist on a well-known saying, objections are often nothing more than a sheep in wolf's clothing. Objections are a sheep in wolf's clothing because objections are usually <u>buying signals</u> *hidden in a comment where it seems the prospect is saying no. Simply put, an objection is often a request for more info, data, time, proof or just a test to see if a salesperson really wants to do business with the prospect,* which can sound like a rejection of you or your product.

When a salesperson is thinking about dealing with objections, he must keep in mind that so much of the reasoning that runs his own personal decision-making processes also runs those of the people he is courting as customers.

Every time consumers go to buy a new or different product or even think about which restaurant to go to for dinner, they go through an evaluation of available information. Switching from a known product or company to an unknown one has an inherent set of risks. For some, even switching shampoo can be a very uncomfortable process.

When a prospect raises an objection, instead of starting to respond, a good salesperson asks questions like, "why do you feel that way?" etc. Ask questions because you may think it's the price, when in reality the prospect has a concern about the product instead or vice versa. Eliminating objections starts back in the evaluation of needs phase.

By working at evaluating prospective clients' needs during the interview stage and matching potential solutions effectively with needs, while using imagination in coming up with some different scenarios that fill the majority of the clients' needs; (price, financing, etc.), objections will be much lighter, if there are any at all. In short, a good interview / evaluation will allow you to custom tailor your presentation, answering most objections before they arise.

Now is the time to think marathon, not sprint. Sprint to a concluding close too fast and the prospect feels rushed. Being pushy with prospects sends up red flags, leaving a lot of room for doubt, and gives them a reason to be especially cautious.

Again, remember that objections are most often a buying signal. In the customer's mind an objection can simply mean: "I am interested in buying but I'm not all *the way there." Perhaps there is not enough relationship, trust, or data to make a decision. The fear of change or the fear of making a bad decision is never far from the prospect's mind.*

These types of concerns and fears are the biggest generators of objections. An objection based on price means "I want it." The prospect is saying, "I'm convinced that it is a good idea to buy this." Now either they don't see the value of the product being as high as the set price or else they have been trained to wrestle for a discount so they can feel good about buying!

A great way of handling objections is to repeat objections back to the prospects, letting them know that they were heard and their concerns are not being ignored. Rephrase a bit or directly repeat the objection. BE CERTAIN TO NEVER, EVER USE "BUT," "NEVER-THE-LESS," "YET," OR ANY OTHER MINIMIZER after repeating their objection back to them. To do so invalidates their concerns and makes it seem like they are being mocked.

The feelings the prospects have just shared as an objection are very real to them. Repeat their objection back to them, pause, and then ask a good question such as, "I am curious, why do you feel that way?" or recognize their situation and work to resolve doubts or issues, such as resolving price concerns with financing options, etc. Just never, ever, allude to the idea that the prospects' objections are anything less than a completely valid observation.

Salespeople get a bad rap for not caring as much about their prospect as they do about themselves. To succeed in relation-ship-based sales, salespeople have to put the prospects' concerns first.

It was the sight of the last journal titled; Closing a Sale, that told Ben it was time for a break. After a long walk around the farm, he stopped into the milk house to revisit the chalkboard and wrote:

"THERE IS A BIG DIFFERENCE
BETWEEN AN OBJECTION
AND A REJECTION!"
-GEORGE PORTERFIELD

Upon his return to the house, he hit the couch to read the daily paper. He awoke with a start at 2:00 a.m. There are a lot of things going on in the world at 2:00 a.m., but not in Springfield Corners. Unable to go back to sleep, Ben decided to watch TV but realized that, since he only had rabbit ears for an antenna, there would be nothing on at this hour.

Then he remembered his laptop. He researched everything from Finlandia Swiss cheese to African safari trips to dating and photos from the Hubble telescope. *"This closing journal will just have to wait,"* he decided, seemingly procrastinating. As dawn nudged its way though the crimson morning sky, Ben fell sound asleep in his recliner with the last journal titled "Closing a Sale" still in his lap.

In the morning he went to the garage and pulled the cover off of his dad's old maroon 1954 Chevy convertible. She had spent a long, cold winter in the barn, but with a quick sponge bath she was ready to run. It was his impending *appointment* with Vernie that raised some much needed excitement about hitting the road to go and get a new outfit or two to wear.

Once inside the department store in Clarksville, he realized he was now on the receiving end of the sales process. And as such, he decided he might as well study it. Within a few minutes of entering the men's casuals department, Marcie, a perky young woman, approached him with a warm smile. "Hello," was all she said as she stopped nearby to straighten up a rack of shirts.

"Hello," Ben said in reply with a wait and see attitude.

Marcie then said, "my name is Marcie. How may I be of service to you?"

And so the process of sales Ben had been studying began to unfold. As Ben saw it, by simply paying attention to who was in her department, she was doing her version of prospecting. Her introduction had been so much more enjoyable, than the bland, "Can I help you?" he usually got.

"I am looking for a new outfit," Ben replied.

Then she asked, "May I ask you a few questions about what kind of occasion the outfit is for?"

"Sure," Ben said with a smile.

"Bingo!" Ben thought. *"She got my permission to ask me questions so that I will feel comfortable answering them."*

Marcie then interviewed Ben about what kinds of clothes he liked and what he was trying to accomplish.

After explaining his upcoming date, she showed him several different outfits ranging from sports casual to "super snappy." When he was looking particularly sharp in one outfit she said, "I think we've got it, don't you?"

Ben then realized this was a trial close, nothing tricky or weird about it, just a rest stop in the conversation to check in to see if they were on the same page.

"I don't know," Ben said. "I don't think it's me."

"This is an objection," he thought. *"I am not actually opposed to buying it, but I'm not yet convinced it's just right for me."*

Marcie ushered Ben to the fitting room mirror. "Look it over for a minute," she said as she rummaged through a stack of magazines. She then showed Ben a photo of Tom Hanks dressed in much the same outfit. Ben smiled brightly, both at being compared to Tom Hanks, whom he adored, and at his ability to recognize her attempt at overcoming his objections.

"It's hard to get a better testimonial for an outfit than Tom Hanks," he said.

Taking Ben's grin to mean that his decision had been made, she simply asked, "Do you like it?"

Ben recognized this question as a concluding close. Meanwhile Marcie waited patiently as he turned around and took a long look.

"Yes, but it's kind of expensive," Ben said just to throw a totally false objection out there for the purpose of his study.

"Yes, it is kind of expensive" Marcie said, smiling. "But it's pretty hard to look like a million bucks for less!"

"I agree," Ben said with a big smile.

They both laughed at that and Marcie informed Ben about a few add-on items like a new belt and some matching shoes.

Ben returned to Springfield Corners via the longest route possible so as to get some much needed time with the wind in his hair. He got home at dusk feeling refreshed. He was so inspired by how simple the process of sales could be, and about the fact that one more whole day had passed, getting him one day closer to Sunday, closer to Vernie. Once settled into his easy chair, he smiled and took a good long look around, it had been a very good day. Finally, he opened the journal titled *Closing the Sale* and began to read aloud:

There are two real kinds of closings, trial and concluding. Trial closes are questions set up along the route of the presentation. Trial closes are like little rest stops along the way to see if the prospect and the salesperson are still on the same page. Trial closes can also be a good way to see if the prospect has any of those dreaded objections.

Trial closes sound like: "How does this sound so far?" What do you think about what I have just told or shown you?" "Do you like the program I've just explained?" Asking these types of questions long before asking for the order is crucial to keeping up "incremental agreements" all along the conversation. It gives the prospects a place to state objections as they feel them. It also keeps them from saving objections up like Kryptonite for the concluding close phase.

Remembering his experience of buying clothes from Marcie, Ben thought about one of the first questions she posed, thinking it was a perfect trial close: "I think we've got it, don't you?"

The journal continued:

> *The concluding close phase is where most salespeople fail by beating around the bush and never actually asking for the order. Looking at sales as a process it's easy to realize that this is the time in the process to ask for the order and fully expect to receive it! Concluding closes sound similar to trial closes and should be a natural conclusion to the presentation. They simply ask, "Are you ready and willing to purchase?" Most important for the beginning salesperson to remember* is to ask for the sale*. Be in the minority who ask and you'll make many more sales than the majority that never do!*

> *Customers need to be asked to buy. After asking for the order, above all else be silent! Let the prospect be the one who speaks next. Silence is uncomfortable for almost everyone, but the longer the silence lasts after asking for the order, the better the chances are that the prospect wants very much to buy.*

Ben recalled his recent purchase again, "Do you like it?" had been Marcie's way of asking for the order. Once he said yes, she was very close to finalizing the sale. Most of the books on sales Ben had read said that you should always ask questions that can't be answered with a yes or no such as, "Should I deliver on Tuesday or Thursday?" Relationship selling is best thought of as always doing what is best for improving your connection with the customer, asking round about questions is something best left undone. Always remember it may take a few appointments or conversations until you get to the opportunity to ask for the order, (concluding close), but in the end be sure you ask for it, sometimes more than once.

> *Again, if the answer to the question, "Are you ready to make this purchase?" is "no," do not be afraid to ask, "Why?" This sounds like: "So I can better understand where you are coming from, why did you say no?" In the answer to this question may lay an opportunity to overcome an objection. At any rate, it will give you a good insight into*

how your product or service is perceived by the prospect.

The dictionary defines closing as: "finishing, concluding, last, or final." It is my opinion that closing a sale is simply the end of a consensual conversation. Without asking for the order you have simply been a professional visitor. Ask, some will, some won't, so what, someone's waiting!

Ben closed his father's journal and took a deep breath. It was midnight. Ben was smiling broadly now as he considered how simple the lessons of selling really were, and how it seemed so natural to want to ask questions and always put the customer first. He also couldn't imagine being afraid to ask for the order ever again.

Even though it was very late, he simply had to get some thoughts and a few of the quotes he discovered during his research written down, so he headed back to his classroom in the barn and wrote:

"REMEMBER THIS IDEA
ALWAYS:

IF YOU DIDN'T HAVE THE
DEAL BEFORE YOU ASKED
AND
YOU DON'T HAVE IT AFTER
YOU ASKED,
YOU ARE THE SAME
AND HAVE LOST
ABSOLUTELY NOTHING."

—BEN PORTERFIELD

"A MAN CONVINCED AGAINST HIS WILL IS OF THE SAME OPINION STILL."

—DALE CARNEGIE

"MOST PEOPLE DO NOT
LISTEN WITH AN INTENT
TO UNDERSTAND.

MOST PEOPLE LISTEN WITH
AN INTENT TO REPLY."

-STEPHEN COVEY

"SUCCESSFUL PEOPLE ASK
BETTER QUESTIONS,
AND AS A RESULT,
THEY GET BETTER ANSWERS."
- ANTHONY ROBBINS

> " YOU CAN GET EVERYTHING
> IN LIFE YOU WANT IF YOU
> WILL JUST HELP ENOUGH
> OTHER PEOPLE GET WHAT
> THEY WANT."
> — ZIG ZIGLAR

Saturday flew by in flurry of activities ranging from cold calling to getting a haircut. Ben was certainly alive again. Even though he was busy with sales activities that now seemed like great fun, Ben's thoughts soon returned to his upcoming date with Vernie.

For Sunday's breakfast Vernie had picked Tubby's Diner in Clintonville as a place to meet. Ben took his time getting ready, taking care to press his new outfit. *"I do look a bit like Tom Hanks,"* he thought with a smile. He fired up the old convertible once again and felt as if she were floating onto the road.

Breakfast with Vernie was absolutely picture perfect. One Sunday breakfast at Tubby's, gave way to lots of picnics, which turned into even more dinners out and walks on the farm. Ben and Vernie became best friends. Like school kids, they would talk on the phone for hours when they had to be apart. She was the woman he had dreamed of sharing his life with, long before he met her.

Two years of courtship and the growth of a solid friendship came about and a wedding date was set. As Vernie and Ben researched an extensive tour of Europe to enjoy the great cheeses and sausages of the world for their honeymoon, Vernie began to fret about the costs of such an extravagance.

"It's time you know the truth," Ben said softly. Vernie's mind raced to her mother's scolding about if things seem too good to be true they probably are. But Ben then said, "I was waiting for the right time to tell you that I closed the Karlsen Foods account! The profit from their first order alone will pay for the whole trip! "

In the end they merged their businesses, and soon Holly Hills Farms stores were featuring Porterfield cheeses along with their line of Holly

Hill's sausages. Soon new stores were popping up all over the place and doing quite well.

There were many more changes in Ben's work life as well. As the chefs and shop owners asked him things they wanted to know about cheese making, not only did he tell them, he sent them articles from his trade publications about making cheese and, new recipes, invited them to his farm, and began to teach classes for them all at Porterfield Farms.

Offering such services to his clients really paid off. He became a trusted partner in their businesses, and soon sales soared even more. One customer nicknamed Ben, "the other cheese.com!" Ben's speaking engagements within his industry were now a big part of what he loved to do. But Ben didn't just speak about cheese. He always kept part of his schedule reserved to speak with students and executives alike about the value of using relationship-based sales techniques.

What Ben had discovered from all his research and hard work was:

The "salesmen" who had originally come by the farm weren't salesmen at all, they were just peddlers. He had realized this because they could care less about what he wanted or needed; in fact, they never even asked. That showed that they were only interested in themselves. He learned that selling was not "soliciting" at all; it was the process of introducing people to products that truly enhanced their lives or businesses.

Asking good questions and always being of service in every interaction with your clients and prospects was what separated salespeople from peddlers, Ben learned. Not only did acting this way make people want to buy from you, but it also made them want to refer you to their friends and colleagues. Ben taught new salespeople to be of service, be patient, be kind, put your client first in all things, and always ask good questions. He also stressed the fact that they had to be absolutely certain to **ask for the order**!

Ben's recollections of his dad's interactions with his prospects and customers still rang out in his mind. "Could you use more specialty cheeses around the holidays?" "What kinds of cheese do the best in sales for you?" "Have you ever tried our Black Dog Cheddar?" George had always been willing to talk with them about storage, aging, and anything else they might ever want to know. George not only gave answers to the questions he knew, he found answers to ones he didn't know.

George's words from the journal filled Ben's thoughts again: "Never be afraid to say; *I don't know* and be willing to go and find out the answer and get back to the prospect."

Ben had discovered you must be willing to be patient when it comes to making a sale. A great many of the *no, thank you(s)* from George's sales calls now buy all their cheese from Ben!

"Some will, some won't, so what, someone's waiting," George's voice rang true in Ben's ears. And hopefully many of Ben's *no, thank you(s)* would buy from his nephew Willy someday in the future.

"Do what you say you will do, when you said you'd do it." George's voice once again rang in Ben's thoughts from his childhood memories. "How hard is that?" George would ask in frustration. In his day, you were expected to honor your word; in later years he felt people didn't care that much about their reputations anymore because they couldn't even return a phone call. "Return your phone calls promptly and follow up with both the people you do business with and those you want to do business with."

"Always remember to follow up on a complaint with action. Even if you have to unwind a sale, it's better than leaving angry customers in your wake. Things are always changing, Ben," George would caution.

Summing up this idea, Ben wrote the final lesson on the milk house wall:

IF YOU DON'T PAY ATTENTION TO YOUR CUSTOMERS, SOMEONE ELSE WILL!

Now it was Ben's turn to continue in his father's tradition and make an entry in the new journal that Vernie had given him.

Succeeding in sales is as simple as introducing yourself to prospects in a friendly way and then asking good questions about their business, while listening with the intention of understanding your clients' needs and how you can be of service by enhancing their lives or businesses. Ask for their business with the certain belief that it is the best thing that can happen to you both.

Once you do business with someone, offer to form some kind of mutually benefi-

cial alliance with them. Offer to be their expert, send them interesting articles or other items of interest. Make it a habit to routinely come by their stores to answer questions from customers during open houses and wine tastings.

For most of his life, Ben had always introduced himself as a farmer. Now when someone asks him what he does, he proudly tells them he is a salesman!

THE GROUP RETURNS

Sonja sat smiling as Tony read the last word of the book aloud. Peter was smiling too. He could see a thirst for learning and the recognition of the value of salesmanship in Sonja. Surely *Gran Alimento* would become a huge success. He was also now excited about getting this little book, *Who Sold My Cheese*, added to the school's required curriculum.

It was agreed at the end of the book reading that, the group would reconvene in six months to see the results of applying the techniques taught in *Who Sold My Cheese*. When the time came, Sonja proudly threw the party for her classmates as she had promised to do and the stories that the group told were incredible.

Using relationship-based selling for Jim's truck accessory business had boosted his sales to the point that he had to hire two new technicians just to keep up with all the new installation work. For Jan, adapting this much more relationship-building approach to sales really paid off. As a result of her increased ability to create relationships, her sales soared, and she was selected New Business of the Year at the National Pet Suppliers Association Convention.

One of the biggest surprises was Tony's story. He came to the incubator as a musician with a dream of opening a shop that sold and rented top end musical instruments. However, reading Who Sold My Cheese showed him that he much preferred sales to operating a business and, he now works for a Piano Company as a sales rep instead.

The biggest change the book made in the lives of the classmates was the realization that sales are a great way to build relationships, as well as a business. They also noted that using a systematic approach to sales, (beginning with the end of closing the sale in mind), was huge in their success stories. Now there was a clear understanding that having a plan was the difference between peddling and salesmanship, and that was everything.

Peter used the lessons of the book for an entirely different reason than the class. Peter's dot com successes meant he no longer needed to pursue money. Instead he thought about how Ben had used these same techniques to find love. With that in mind he began to think about Sonja in a completely different light. While this sounds a little like a May-December romance it really wasn't as Peter is only eight years Sonja's senior.

Adding a relationship-based sales approach to these small businesses was not only key to their survival, but also their meteoric rise in their respective fields. For the rest of the class, the addition of this book's information had a huge impact on their individual bottom line.

The moral of the story is that success in relationship-based sales isn't a huge thing; it's a lot of little things!

The End

Wrapping It Up

I hope you have enjoyed this opportunity to understand sales and the selling process. The secret however is not only in understanding these lessons but in applying them. "Do or do not, there is no try" is a quote made popular by the Star Wars character YODA.

When you apply these lessons to your daily activity, you will succeed where others have failed. Just as in the book there is a directive to be the one who asks for the order, action is all-powerful.

And we're here with training and guidance by offering: Consulting, coaching and onsite workshops tailored to your individual needs. If you have any questions about how to use the processes in this book feel free to email me.

If you are with a particular company and would like to have a version of this book customized to fit your company's unique identity, please contact me.

www.WhoSoldMyCheese.com

info@whosoldmycheese.com

763-688-1628

10 a.m. to 6 p.m. (Central Time)

Quick Order Form

Email: info@whosoldmycheese.com

www.whosoldmycheese.com

PLEASE NOTE: Credit card orders paypal accepted.
http://www.WhoSoldMyCheese.com

Postal orders pay by check made out to: Inspired
Directions Publishing and mail to: **Inspired Directions
Publishing** 14329 Barton Ave., Monticello, MN 55362

Please send more FREE information about:

☐ Other Books   ☐ Speaking and Seminars

☐ Other _____

_____

Please send me:

_____ *Who Sold My Cheese!* @ $12.95 ea $ _____
add $5 shipping and handling for 1 or 2 books.
Please contact me for additional shipping charges. MN
residents add 6.5% tax.
Quantity discounts available on special request. Contact
info@whosoldmycheese.com for more information.

Name: _____

Address: _____

City/State/Zip: _____

_____

Phone: (   ) _____

Email: _____